Raw Skies

Also by Nigel Wheale

Answerable Love (Great Works Editions, 1977)
Simples (The Many Press, 1979)
Strong Lines Recessional Numbers (infernal methods, 1980)
The Plains of Sight (The Many Press, 1989)
Remote Sensing (Poetical Histories, 1989)
Phrasing the Light (The Many Press, 1994)

with Walid Abdul-Hamid
He Said to His Prince and Patron Sayf Al-Dawla (Poetical Histories, 2002)

The Postmodern Arts: An Introductory Reader (Routledge, 1995)
Writing and Society: Literacy, Print and Politics in Britain 1590-1660
(Routledge, 1999)

As editor
Shakespeare in the Changing Curriculum (with Lesley Aers) (Routledge, 1991)
Remaking Shakespeare: Performance Across Media, Genres and Cultures (with
Pascale Aebischer and Edward J. Esche) (Palgrave Macmillan, 2003)

Raw Skies

New & Selected Poems

Nigel Wheale

Shearsman Books
Exeter

First published in the United Kingdom in 2006 by
Shearsman Books Ltd
58 Velwell Road
Exeter EX4 4LD

www.shearsman.com

ISBN-10 0-907562-75-2

ISBN-13 978-0-907562-75-7

Acknowledgements: see pages 146–147.

The publisher gratefully acknowledges financial assistance from
Arts Council England.

CONTENTS

The Plains of Sight (1989)

As if from the Russian (1986)

Strong Lines Recessional Numbers (1980)

J : tibi seruiat ultima Thule

I sent a tightly folded poem, expecting no reply.
Your answer came, woven in the tide's race,
The wordless speech of branches.

Flows and Traces

2003

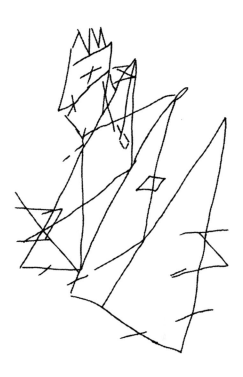

Curlew Glide

Rises stuttering, a seeded trail of cries
flung between the green and the grey,
he marks his ground in song spraint.

At full curve from tail to beak tip,
wing blades flexed,
the arc of song
tense with an urgency we seem to know
thrills to a joyful alarm.

In the clearing of night
they are homeless star cries
stitched upon soft felt.

Riddle

Rapid breaths across the wan dome.

Sheddings of light from an ice-pleated sky.

Wave upon pulse, a shiver among stars.

White satin sheet, furrowed and stained.

Breathing of sand across dark dunes.

Fumes of light, snagging on Algol.

A weaving drape of light-fall

thrown down to this earthline.

Goose Field

A gentle inbreath as two hundred wings
unfold to beat them upwards. Once there,
they fade to strandlines, crying creatures
strung out against the northern light.

Gull-motes surf above the latten-grey Flow,
buoyantly underlit. Fierce masses of water
trade gradients below. Soon Draco
will fracture their sky with his bright graph line.

O sleep, thou fleshly birth, may you
never be free of your heart, here
in a world that the world might make.

A night endless like the sea's waves . . .

A night endless like the sea's waves, a dark curtain flooding,

bringing the sky-host of anxieties.

I said, as it arched its huge back above me,

its chest unmoving, the hips so far beyond,

'Monstrous night, make way for dawn,

though morning will bring no relief.

Such a night you are, as if your stars

were tied to the Ward Mountain by thick chords,

the Pleiades bound with simmans to rock.'

From the *Mu'allaqa* of Imru'al-Quays (lived 497–545 AD; a pre-Islamic poet from Najd, Yemen. Translated with Walid Abdul-Hamid.

Flow Stone

Trending layers swept south
      across the intermontane basin,
'a sea gradually shallowing'
      gently deposed blank pages of rock
Over millennia, pressing rare life.
Now stone-frozen fish swim the strata
      within lamina of grey mudshale.

Glazed by light in a moment's breath,
      a wave's feathering
Is caught across warm silt skin.
      Now it is rock-woven,
Eve's falling tresses at Autun
      drift on the palaeocurrent.

Then flexures, folding and faulting
      contort the passive sediment.
Firths and straits are overdeepened
      under glacial stress,
Mountains levelled and gouged
      and all is overlain
By thin tills of glacial drift.

At Outertown the basal complex
      is laid bare, granite flesh
Shot with white banding,
      dykes become shattered rubble.
Thermal aureoles burn within the granite
      to survive this savage downthrow,
Cold rock under the sparagma of stars.

Wind Huis

There are breeze ghosts in the wind slabs
when near-gales burnish stone and flesh alike.
Window songs and chimney voices
pluck at the soul of the small hours,
peedie ones dancing maniacally beyond the wall's depth
under the glancing loom of the lighthouse.

This house begins to sing once more,
tuning for long winter,
but by morning light-quiet has been won
between the passage of storms,
a front losing its identity beyond the Fair Isle,
morning a solvent of warming light,
and silence wide as the bay curves to the hills.

Small birds make nests
in branches high against the sky.
Their song hangs open to the light
as all of time begins to brim
towards the corners of our day.

Such a scale of light

Such a scale of light
soothed the islands last evening
under a bird-calling stardome.

Morning's glarestrip is laid upon the waters,
turquoise of inshore plunging to dark
over the hundred fathom deeps.

Quick flecks move on the bay below
as a whitemaa cloud rises from the back rig,
sown by spring's harrow.

Swiftless these skies, light spaces aching
for wing notes, heart cries of young May,
gracing the bitter sharp savours of hoar thorn.

Yet two buds upon each sprig
have made the mountain blush
across the bay.

Sea Notes

There are no tricks in sea painting,
no short cuts to success as a sea painter.
I intend to analyse waveform through my responsive medium,
sweeping in the main lines with a flowing brush of thin Ivory Black.
Too much detail would suggest the sea stood still to be portrayed.

First lay in the semi-dark waveforms.
In this way the immensity of the sea
rolls through the carrying power of the colour.
The rocks will show their resistance to the sea.
The water, though enormous in mass, is pliant.

You must work at top speed, placing
everything on canvas in its proper value,
leaving accidentals in the mixed tone.
These will reflect a greater sense of light.
The canvas begins to have colour all over
and your highlights should flash like amber drops,
more brilliant than foam.

Rose Madder purples shadow colour,
detracting from the sunlit detail.
It is not lack that blooms in the shadow,
only reflected light.
In this case, a pink note runs throughout.

You could not paint a landscape sky
into a seascape work. There is more halation
by the sea. The clouds are more radiant
in tone and colour. The peep of the sea below
provides a platform of complementary colour.

A certain amount of wildness
is apparent in this rough note.

Formulas lightly adapted from Borlaise Smart, *The Technique of Sea Painting* (1946).

Five Remarks about Waves

Waves leave no mark upon each other
but have certainly impressed these redstone cliffs.

The luminous inner palm of which wave was it
has left these Spanish detergent bottles
ecstatically high at the driftline?

All of those frail waves have carried all of those great ships.

The wave passes through its medium
like a persuasive idea, vertically agitating
all the stationary monads, itself unmoved.

Nature's way of bringing the sea to an end,
waves are not symbols of permanence or change,
nor of passion or equanimity.
The Department of Wave Mechanics knows this,
but will never be able to convince the oceans,
forever fretting at the land.

Surface Tension

A meniscus skins water
with transparent rigour.
Creatures walk upon it
or fail to pierce it
from beneath,
condemned to water.

This inter face curves
from shore to shore,
a sac dividing anti worlds.

Waters meeting across a temperature gradient
struggle to level their surface differences,
the meniscus line a complex polymer
ferociously dancing as it arbitrates.

At middle dusk the water face
petulantly throws off light of the sky
and its depths withdraw
under implacable grey.
Small insects touching on this silvered flesh
fall through, but do not sink.
The face of the water eats them via its creatures.

Fight or Flight

Racing tidal headwaters
etch an eroding shore.
Each stone and wrack stands clear
in a raking daedal dawn.

Light's seven-braided blade
hangs above the brae,
fierce covenant of times to come.

How you walk the wastes of this heart,
the sharp tang of our flowering
still upon me.

Sea Glance

Sea mews open forever inward
at a drift line beyond the ocean traffic surf.

A lightfall crosses a beckoning hand
and bright sadness turns like pebbles in water.

Your tides of hair in the wave are watered silk
over-broken by our furling breast of human happiness.

Against whom, Rose

Against whom, Rose,
have you assumed such thorns,

Sweet as herb and clover
after sea crossing,

Potent as smoke
of quicken wood fire,

Patient as limpet's kiss
corroding rock
over one thousand years?

Him I love purely as bird skull

Him I love purely as bird skull
washed white by raw tides.
Him I love throughly as cliff
pierced by salt seas.
Him I'll take to the dream-stall,
sleep's byre, love's kist.
Lying between pelts and fern,
thralled by rock, there we shall share
night and the kisses that melt stone.

Sea Hallow

Was there ever such light
as we walk this Souls' Way
from Tuquoy to the Cross Kirk,

Our subtle and winding mass road,
starred and burned
with tormentil and the day's eye.

Off Congesquoy otters work
the fish-bearing tide. Covens of eider deplore
the trend of the times as sea-sure fulmar dare us to fly.

All across this gambler's scatter of isles
great breathers gaze over wire, backroundin beasts,
impassive, batch-numbered by their yellow ear-tie.

Among the working planes of the tidal race
the in-curving swirl of a turbine shell
catches at the breath of waves for light.

The moon's love for earth shoals these waters around us.
High winds fill the heart's chamber, the hills arch once more,
great cats flexing to a fierce hand's stroke,

For there is never such light
as when we walk the margins
of this gate to oceans beyond sight.

In the serene of evening

In the serene of evening
as the light darkens
the sun may choose
a field, a house, a landspar,
and give it light, give such light,
that the enclosed garth stands free,
and we see how people may live
upon this world, so clear,
in that moment when the steadings
shine under low sweeping light,
and a settled life seems to be sown
across the braes and the fallow lands.

Yet the terminal flare rages tonight
in the smallest hours
as the year begins to tilt
down to the long dark,
the birds now quiet
when in spring
they were so clamant,
the bay wind-furrowed, fretted
with urgent white waters.
Fierce Mars has courted the Moon
these six nights, and the Moon
now refuses to wane, stands proud,
scattering her prodigal glow,
a rolling tract between the working sea-lights,
her moonpath overlaying them, direct to each eye.

There are tracks that lead down to the sea,
that must end at the shore,
a margin bulwarked with rock armour,
breeze block, broken cement rubble,
against the rising chaffing infeasible waters,
yet the light runs down to the sea.
Wind lines weave over grass staves,
signing their passage. Hare tippets
peak above the sea of waving greenness,
the fields a wet pelt under rain.

And there are nights when
all that is to be seen are four house lights,
one star hanging on the mist-wall,
the haar veil, mist's truth against sight.
Everything now flowers, unfolds from here,
all that may be said, from love's place.

In the half-time after the time

Their pelts warm in the late raking sun
and they prick their tippet ears then break ground
unharried and fleet beyond reason

We balanced at dew point in the dell
wefts catching sunfall over grass-bents
starred bryony in the ragged carr

As your nape was furred under total light
bird motes swarming and stalling above us
when love cast beyond the defences.

Star Shot

Beyond the floor strewn with rushes
a door brim, the whitening hold-thresh,
above us the sharp-down slabs of dark
moistened by interstellar gleam.

There lost in the complete seriousness of a hazel pupil,
an eye-white now shadowed by life,
latticed with thought, allhallown,

Let fall the sash frame to drink
our cool of night, freshened by the wall's rough harl,
voices of new water barely beyond.

Notes

Island Words

Back rig : plough ridge
Backroundin : cattle tail-end to the rain
Haar : sea mist
Harl : rough cast
Kist : chest
Peedie : diminutive
Quicken wood : rowan tree
Simmans : braided heather rope
Whitemaa : gull

page 15: 'a sea gradually shallowing' from Hugh Miller, *The Old Red Sandstone; or, New Walks in an Old Field* (1850), page 67.

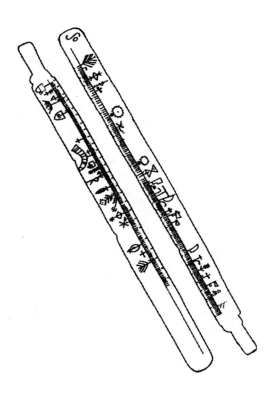

Hearing and Calling

1999

A Night Piece

The light is voice-activated.
The car-alarm is fear-activated.
The door is seriously alarmed.
The massing swifts are season-activated.
The moon is light-activated with cloud voice-overs.
The tides are moon-activated.
The garden is drought-infested.
The pet is food-activated.
The politics-alarm is boredom-activated.
The love-alarm is word-, breath-, heat- or sweat-activated.
The guidance system of the massing swifts is star-activated.
They fly blind, and blindsight serves them.

They feel the pressure falling well in advance,
and take off on the maps they've laid down
over several years, quartering terrain
that we would never recognize.
Hundreds of miles in open sea, landfalling
at this moustache of pine trees top of the northern coastline.
Oh and you have to flyby the bombing ranges too,
which are urgently hunting possible new targets these days,
weapons mis-named 'smart' quartering the contours
with onboard Ter-con software.

But if your skeleton is shot through with air-sacs
and you weigh less than three ounces then you register
and internalize barometrics, you are coterminous
with the breathings of the large-scale schemes,
the very heart of the air-system is within you,
your breast your wings, and your heart your mind is
a systolic pressure lifted by the advance and retreat
of weather fronts – but not at all Michael Fish,
nor is your weather report sponsored. Feet
you hardly have any, who needs them,
tedious extensions of little use for covering the ground,
all you need is something which orients you
for the few occasions when you touch down,
something with which to plash the nest materials,

in due course attend to eggs, maybe sketch out
an enigmatic courtship diagram
on the white sand of a dune's breast.

There is a phase of walking on this front line,
In the mid-late evening during November for example,
when you might know what it is like to fly without reference.
Everything is melded, occluded, elided, there is no ground,
this if ever any thing was is groundlessness,
and the air and dark are a new medium
like velvet opening before and closing behind you.
The night breathes you. Stars touch cigarette flares
deep within your pulmonary sacs. Is this
pleasure or complete dereliction.
Counting paces seemed like a sensible idea
to begin with but becomes too prudent
and is thrown overboard, and so
you might walk gratefully into the countless.

Love has not been enough,
its wings have been not trimmed
but how shall I say superseded,
so that we find our selves
on the far side of love for the first time,
but still stricken at heart, still full-winged
in the key of hope for it.
Which permeates us as weather,
and strikes us through, so that
we do rise above it and extend our selves
to the other

Living Quietly

The weeks and months make their returns
by indemnifying, adding to the sum.
Bird clouds inflect each risen day
which arrives with a customary candour,
and light insinuates for ever
around the edges of the door.

The dreams we step out of, pains of the night,
have once again been concerned with journeys
through landscapes where we have never been
but which are as familiar to us
as our lives seen through turbid water.
And they are released into the forms of present living
through manifold pressures long ago laid down.

On such mornings everything becomes clear –
the general brushwork clarifies –
and we are freed by the loosening of those strict bands
wound so firmly around our upper chests.
Stepping into the kitchen, everything is to hand,
the salt and pepper, and next them a blended honey,
the slicing knives, cups at ease on the blue glaze tiles.

They call into their names
as if this all were a guarantee of nomenclature
which could only and for ever be such:
but Eternity will not be added to,
stands wide apart, as do stars from earth.

Towards the end of summer
implacable hardness of the road extends
to each horizon
as the world's moment rings under the tension
of a plate glass window overstressed, threatening to convex
into streets far below, crowded with children
returning home from successful music lessons.

Criticality becomes localized
at the turn of every stair
haunted by enigma: gears crash
and whatever it was continues to shake us
either from within or from without.

In that hard August, full of stencilled shadow
and specimen days, it was surely you, Tian,
down on the foreland,
placating the spirits of torn-up letters.

We always knew it, retreating to our naked bed,
savaged by rainwinds and starry breastmilk light.

Silent Coast

The clouds above are established
and below are the fountains of the deep:
within their clear waters a face
may brokenly answer to a face.
The streaming constellations
offer an almost language:
and our skies issue cold noise
as the inner life of happiness,
which seems to fall from planets
desperate as our selves:
they turn upon each other
and are pursued with bitter glee:
emptily they reach, as emptily embrace,
at a demented limit.
Above and below this world's ridge
the pure fires shine, set about by working, disintegrating seas.
In a sublime and fiery bliss of interstellar gender
the heart exults from depths of the inward body,
a restless muscle, not knowing any better.
How many times the earth has been erased
from the face of sky.

What is it that damasks the waves of this great bay
as if with a care for each moment within the deep sad systems
of the sea? Stone crop flares on the boulder face
and we walk the high edge, our words leaving no mark,
silent on the more general silence. The great sun
is absconded beyond the waste and we navigate as if
we were the old-time sailors, peering eyelessly to gain
the pressure of invisible land with a facial seeing,
the blind sight of those who move by dark of intuition
and the common surface of the skin.

Trailing void radar signatures,
dream boats continue to pass each other in the night,
just as daytime is figured by ghostly dazzle ships
which sail in search of the lost papers on consciousness,
eyes transpersant through the main sea deep.

It is the blank mirror of our deeply refracted day,
light snagged in the countless heads of grass
between which we move as a loosened congregation,
above the great sea pulling west to intractable cold
of the ocean roads.

But now, the glancing visits of low December light
upon the house side, the foreshore stones, your face
and all that might be seen: now from the valleys
for which we once were grateful the striking chill
more cold than could have been known,
black trees shot through by hoar glow.
This is the country of unknown grammars,
of states of the verb so intricately forward flung,
and which brace about upon a distant pastness, subjunction:
about a dark mid-point of time are balanced this year and the next,
while history lies scattered like garden-centre seed
across the patio flags and hard-standing.
Now the moon is full and we cast no shadows on it,
she gives a light we would not qualify:
the array of stars offers an infinity of hope
but when the nightly plain of dreams falls aslant,
how much of it is for us?

Yet on our return, everything is quiet,
for the moment, we explore the room
as if for the first time. It had been described to us
time and again but that is never any preparation,
any induction to the absolute change that being here makes.
The weather of the room is now temperate, even dreamy,
and this too rocks us back, after those stormier early passages.
On the shelves are poems and novels full of heart calligraphy,
and outside there is a morning of quite complete openness,
as next door's child steps into it, saying words
which it has never even heard before,
making that kind of progress which is slightly beyond itself,
pointing brightly to that which is taken to be its face.

All Is True, or, What You Will

It's been getting colder again
a little deeper every time
the perfume evaporating a touch more slowly
from the inner fore-arm, pearlizing the skin
with a degree even of reproof.
Each dawn the birds hunt through,
hawking and singing, bashing the keys
with fistsful of codesong.

Then it is love turns to watered music,
notes spreading silent over litmus.
Faces of incompletion half-awake
to the gift of the kiss of consciousness,
filmed eyes committing themselves to blurred fields
but seeing no line through the Black Wood at Madron.

There are times when I've loved the weight
of this silence, and will again, but for now
it is also the presented fact of vacancy,
gwavos – the winter homestead of a life.

Sloe gin braids and chords as it falls to the glass,
a red that has swallowed blue.
Wine and pigment have bled to running water
of a borderless river, dyes that separate and drain,
veiling and blinding across the membrane's arcane white.
Where was the silk also watered and double-turned?
There where rhyme fringed the blood like frost.

Between the houses dwell raggedly agitated trees,
green as verbs, curving russianly
under air's promiscuous love.
Poplar forever combs her hair into the given;
birch stands aloof and seriously filters the sky.
Wittily each flock streams in unity
over earth's lip;
manoeuvre waves thrill each contingent.
We smile upon the four-footed ladies
heavily browsing their fields.

Then it is our catchlights diffuse
in a prevailing light spill
and we are entered by weather,
rim-lit, eye line to eye line,
and who would be otherwise.

Young marrieds, ardent as suburbs,
cruising the shelf stacks,
all is before you, quickening
like nape down in the brisk air!

Whose action is no stronger than a flower

Through Amalwhidden of the pale slope
      and serious alder
to Bos-ygrane headland where there was
      beauty in the rocks.
The grasses were an arm's down
which catches the morning light
and the figure becomes more than flesh.
A white court and its more white sorrow
      had long since scattered
with isotopes drifting in at the sea line
and Ireland reserves itself
      behind the interface of sky.

Something like a slight long wave
that has travelled several oceans
      had broken within you,
and now withdraws, leaving the shingle readjusted,
      but no one could say how.
The granite lies where it once burned and cooled,
brushed by a pelt of ochre lichen
      and shell-green fur,
glowing residually through its heavy duty grass.
Myriad umbels of wild carrot swathe the headland
and in the hollow of the promontory,
a moment of the collar bone not yet become neck,
pale manes of sedge blush and sigh
as earth's last expression
      before air takes over.
Ruined towers of digitalis
      tipped with the last remaining flowers
are raggedly angled to sky, desperately purple,
imprudent as blooded florets of heather
which intensify the grain of the cliff's shoulder,
a fierceness given for being at the edge of things:
it is the reckless glimmer of a peacock's wings
closed up against too much sun, suddenly gaping
to be dusted by weightless light.

A frame has been placed around event,
every sequence is now edged by a serious rim:
noontide shadows of the tree with cows
in a field's middle distance
darken to cobalt, their under-painting
lost to sight. No precise emotional value
attaches to any of this, except for
vague disquiet and a sisterly elation
which can be called upon through having gained
this clearer sense of the total. Cheque-stub days.

I'd rather tell you now about these tiny effects,
like the disconcerted flight of a meadow brown
which havers and threatens to fall from the air,
an oak chip blown upward on the fire's draught,
than cruel platitudes which don't bear the hearing:
for the hollowing sky stands between poplar and birch,
and that which is irreplaceable shines out
from the palmate and the serrate leaves.
        Love thorn, thunder tree,
        Turn whitely on your life bone to me.

Outwith

A world of air breathes generously
        intimately across pages, forearms, cots
Through quiet rooms where curtains pull
        pale against half-open windows
In concert with the door against its jamb
        and young parents grow into themselves
Waiting on whispered voices
        via the nursery intercom.

Beyond the dusty glazing bars
        fistsful of swallows
Have been dashed in face of early August —
They don't fly, exactly, nor do they sing
        but will leave a ghost refrain
On the emptied staves of phone lines
        by September, soon.

Lilac over a burnished blade
        this cityscape sky
With traffic running like hectic in the blood
        nervewine baying at you
Past vastly scaled-up homesteads
        of wall- and tile-tracts over voids
Filled with food from far away
        as world shyness rates
Go hungrily through the roof.

A cassette tape stream
        snagged in roadside grasses
Catches lights from the flow
        song cast free of the spools
Like Rachel sighing
        for her kerbside floral tributes
A fireweed spread along arterial routes
        waving and scorched in backdraught

As a scend of transparent water breaks
      across our woodfall canopy
Over the sele of day and this darkening breast
      tasting again the firstness of things
For love of the hours and their openness
      where the longer waves pulse on
            Crested still by fore-edged tongues.

At the Brim

Light in the cappella void
where music is human glass
every line and voice glazed by echo
and the damp song of stone,
O five-toned human sound.

Modal, sea star,
a gendered voice
moves through the halls
of each chambered heart
gradual by note and syllable

      Electa
            Chosen
     Effectua
           Proven

Fruit of our side how is it
we filled you with diverse love
as you raided with a child's merciless need
and took the word straight from our skull
which we were minded to speak,

As birds have left the halves of egg shells
redundant and fragile on the grass
their blue superfluous and calling to sky,
up to which they have thrown fledged creatures?

At Wild Hope

Her stone is in fawn against time.
You hear the air cut by wing-swift flight.
In their slipstream a skygash is left singing.

The doe-eyed ones move in a frame beyond us.
Clouds are staged as for the Stranger's arrival.
Trust that the well is not poisoned against you.

Upland Houses

Who could not want the upland houses?
They float on a measureless rock blanket
accented with tongues of igneous intrusive.
Bright and generous norms of light fall on them
among the high old amphitheatres of pressure ice.

Each is a house of secrets, corners set
by a six-man stone: they are the obligations
under which we live, none of them known,
and none inert:

They circulate among us, themselves a kind
of individual, generating intimacy and fear
as at each gift battle we meet in closeness
which is an equal and opposite distance.

Throated stars and the power of clouds
invest their boundary: they are the rim
of this present world, for which we must

Descend again, carried by a gentle largactyl flow
back to the valleys of police mysticism,
the dictionary cities. There too is the Asking Festival.

Landscape with a Calm

The high altitude rock-to-cloud transfer
operates with customary glide and grace,
denying substance. In the valleys below
tonal handling reduces human incident
to pure formality. Foliage maddens
and only light is opulent,
melting the frail works of stone.
Bless the anonymity of silence,
where we are barely figured.

But the room ideally displays them all,
co-opted and tensed between its walls and apertures.
The columns bear, the walls divide and part,
a floor upholds, as in the ceiling
reflected light defines the empty upper air
where ribboned swags of everlasting green
are more than architectural.

They kneel towards a love, she profiled,
gullible and knowing, opposed by the seated priest;
her husband centrally, his hand that hovers
like the spirit, like a bond, sealing her prayerful gesture,
the priest endorsing by an underhand subvention.

The couple meets alone,
their teams of gendered players
line out like a badly shaken cocktail party
on either side of the room.
The single transgressing presence him on the left,
golden from invisible light, —
who does he think he is?

His shadow falls obliquely over everything,
only the bride's head and shoulders rising
like a grateful seal to air above his darkness.
And between the column and the window's soffit,
half-seen, an unknown grace remains reserved and draped.

Tough Love

And it's follow vigorous water cuts
of the burn at back of the mountain
up through the shaling lower skirts,
cross the blank ground of upper slopes
and so delight in the throat flung back
to the skies of the corrie falling on you.

Pitch in the afterglow of the northern day
lighter in the dusk than we can know,
run-off coursing slight and peat-inflected,
fed from the overlay which shortly crashes
on the dry ridges above. Water voices
are here still, persistent, just beyond sense.

This cradled pleasure of the high corries,
at midnight the sky washed blue,
and the sporadic flares of major stars breaking,
tentative in solar winds, a bland skydome
which tests yer shaking hand, the sweat cooling
as ye try to pull focus on the new first star
dodging about in the perfectly shaped miasma
of heat-mist rising on the wind plumes
and sculpted by the funneling breaths
from the corrie walls above, a hindenberg,
an enskyed trident, a thought-balloon
observing the decorum of the mountain line.

The formal pitch of loveliness is still beyond you,
sweating fool, awkward, glancing and broken
as a russian sonata, a trustful flaring waystar.

Wake from a rough ocean of sleep
and take pleasure in the falling sound of rain,
wine of the hills, rain wines,
drink of the air and running waters,
the new green clamant, the older trees soughing,

You turn my breath and heart
like the openness of a moral face
which makes you strange to the world.

New York/Warsaw Transfers

1991

The Africans Selling Gucci on the Avenue
of the Americas

Our jetstream gathers the flag-blue eye-blue light,
and a manic rule is laid to the star cup,
those infinitely hidden lights and numberless thresholds
within the high currents of the oceanic crossing.
Night weighs on the right wing as on the left
the sunset lightslick rolls across impermeable cloud,
                        and we yet above
jacked via our arm chair
into some Dutch comedy show on Channel #12,
Meryl Streep the phantasmal in-flight She-Devil.

Our 747-400 series is named 'Tear of the Cloud',
and has suffered only two careful drivers, while eleven k. below
on the old mayflower route Anne Bradstreet makes out
among sporadic iceflows with her 400 companions.

Touchdown, given free choice but no quarter
we opt for the phrase shift
and a cold electric smash kicks in at the pineal gland
like plate-glass love over frost,
the taste of this neon song we've been hearing all our lives,
                        'Cruising America'.
Welcome to the land of dead marilyns
where terrible men stand upon the shores
and play the nested game of the names of the New.

Mordants acid-etch the city's circuit board and we are
gridlocked into fierce raptus by the high stacked money
the punishing wealthy beauty of Manahattan's rigor –
offences of height and gilt, cash and glazes
from which nothing falls excepting the street dead
who fell way before the first fence
in the exiled wombs of inconsequent mothers.

All those failing conspicuously to be persons
                        the under-lovers
remaining bound within and beneath the law of things
and the black urine of Grand Central

shooting up in human blood all round the orbed concourse,
the Moderne swathed in nets of restoration
where a shtetl lament drifts upside down and covert within
a jazz soprano sax working the Metro-North commuter masses.

Where street gamblers take thin bills from the lonely masses
and compassion is read as routine harassment.
Where only the daintily drifted steam heat
run over perpetually by yellow cabs
rises again above the dimes and knuckle bones punished
into molten asphalt, glazed with the burnt sugar smoke
of each pretzel stand.

Over the #37 channel night-waves the police-death of children
is sung within hours here where crime is the common civility,
the absent term for the shared commonality,
a flag-glazed violent fear.

And it began to rain a grey color
brushing us too into the asphalt at the Dont Walk junction
when we were hustled by another paper cup
and an exigent circumstance rising from her cardboard
at the steel curb, crushed by the unresponsive cabs
the blanket case who wished us happy easter from behind her
                                    proffered need.

High overhead satellite passes note the greed heat bloom
of the marble slopes which usher us down to the running wall
where you can fight for bankrupt headscarves
in the Mall of the Fat Americas.
But as to who has franchised the eyeless subservience
of the blacks touting watches from cardboard boxes
on the Avenue of the Americas
                                    they are silent
among nested lights.

Luminitsa

Dark money waves continually overrun a shoreless country,
storms raised by the Union of Descendants from a vivid past.
It is filth dust from the thin soil,
recalcitrant sand whose grass will not suffer to be walked on,
raised also by ghost turbulence in the laminated airs
and the privilege of having been a targeted nationality.

The east is still dark at night and in cities
heavy on the heart-chest with a diesel miasma
which strips out inner linings
the Gray Ranks materialize on the instant
in any cinema or food queue
at drop of a regretful gesture.

Peoples are on the move again,
suitcase merchants from Kirghizia
and Rai great lord king of the Roma
swallows golden obols at the frontier.
Inept travellers stranded in way camps
provoke the folk custom of wired enclosures.

During forty years there was nothing to do,
people went dissident from boredom mostly.
But of his palace it is still said
there are more rooms below the soil than above,
more windows than five years of laborious days
and never counted the same
where mothers' sons and daughters vanished
into the one-way mirror of surveillance
as beyond the gate women made the great curse
holding their block-print headscarves against the sun.

If taken, you recited your works
to the audience of captors
only to preserve them,
and desire was writ bitter in lemon juice.

[No permission has been given to reflect on this verse]

You rise before me the paleness
still on you
the lake of tears at our feet
you breach the veil of their curtain
my partisan love
the bright blind screen you offer me
my song of ascent
a delicate forum over wire over walls
in the birch glade
to which each shall bring an opened palm of egg shells

Altman's House

Memorial text-light hallows the doorpost:
she shines above the lintel
whose threshold is entry
to this undeceiving place.

Pomegranate and souffrance cup,
knifeless by the densely woven wooden plates
with flower and bird of the given.

They live the life of tents,
invisible canopy on which is plaited
schemes of clear propriety and love.

And on the children's shelf
the family of dolls is safely boxed:
within their hollow painted forms
lies the true and hidden family of dolls.

Creaturely, the scent of horse,
sweeter than perfume.
Their goat's eye as frank as a moon
of first blessing.

Scarcely above the pale
the life of frosted stars
shawls colour-meaning,
as if in care of this.

Aniol

Living creatures run and return
across the loading square

where the birds who sing with meaningless dedication
are silent, but only in myth.

The perpetrators fitted devices at the angelic heart
of this event, and it is not understood,

amber fires infolded against human sense,
the terrible ice of heat and bitterness.

AmEx overrides the pitiful local dust money
and sandsoil drifts
into the blonde falls of political moustaches and ashen hair.

If style could save us then we would not have died long ago,
We pictures looking strangely on pictures of the strange.

Selekcja

A selection of enamelled names
is nailed to the whitened bole
of the dead tree at Pawiak,
where parade ground
cancels play ground.

To raise the light which cools
you must derive equally paced from here,
and this may clear the air ways.

The branches may bend low with their fruit
but still you will not know
which the bitter and which the sweet.

Black Thorn

Yeast bloom on the bullace
bright among your murder thorns
a blue that calls with bitterness.

Olives of the north light,
sad grapes, wineless plum
we'll burn you with rime-frost

Before we're done.
Then darkly gather your darker sweetness
and extort the blue-red life of wine.

The earth seemed unearthly

Novalis and I were hang-gliding the walls of data
on petroleum thermals that rose from traffic canyons far below,
collating cloudtop with seasurface,
scanning through our landsat high tensity regard
all that viral writing across insufferably thin architecture
matte entablatures, beige pilastering, no white.
Novalis had the lightest keyboard touch, never known to mis-key
and his formatting was integral song to the degree of depth.

The clouds were flowing bronze across transnational surfaces
and no one could touch us try as they may
when we scooped drink from office fountains,
nipped hibiscus blooms from the boss plant
and dropped them pale
behind the surprised ears of brisk telephonists.
At night the office mesa walls turned outward
with a striplight permaflow that signed executive messages
of hopeless love to distant wives in Stepford.

Cruising this detritus of politicians and their shoreline shit
we were frisking the current Catastrophe Theory buzz
compellingly in circulation: that the weightless reflex
of a butterfly wing within the total sum might take us over
a blissful event horizon. Nach we paid no heed.

Was this to be the choice of life?
Command activity clustered ever more fiercely
below the surface and was keeping strictly low-dimensional.
GOLDEN HELLOS ricocheted between rock-like facades
of all those imperturbable banks whose green-screens
color up on narco-dollar snorts. But it's a LEADEN GOODBYE
to north of the border which now lacks all mandate
and no writ running, where government slavers like a human dingo.

Sealed cities, banned funerals
and caspars hold the inner perimeter
steel-sighted under sodium arcs.
Night-long the washing of death shrouds
and their proving in dawn winds.

But me and Novalis kept on heart-flogging
through all this New Age crime,
forgetful of the hollow muscle's risk,
him on the higher road and me on the hard shoulder,
looking for some facial disk of living waters.

Till we found her, darkened with the movement of flocks,
scarred and notated by myriad shopping feet
intent on their transgressive consumption,

She is a pavement artist's crayon cartoon,
study in sanguine heightened with white
and more of this earth colour it is not possible to be.

Your outer island hair streams upward from the testing winds of love
as we shoal in your skirts, flight-singing involuntarily
like Tienanmen pigeons, flute-tubes drinking the sweet air
                                        at our pouting breasts.

Arroyo Real

In the high-tensity gallery case
gold foil leaves on an ancient alexandrine lover's crown
shiver to the skip of a far-down seismic beat.

Lean stealth-swallows vector thru haze
hanging at edge of the waves' teeth
          on the slide, on the slip
snorting volatile chaparral oils,
          keyed-up on air tone
over degrading quartzite earth,
          updraughting on subalpine bliss
gifted from the color-blushed peaks above,
delicate as faded frescos gracing a by-passed Diner.

Self-possessed night waves pulse to the bay shore
like veins moving under darkened indian skin
over which free-loading surfers busk in dayglo suits
sporting ditzy miners' lamps at bronzed foreheads.
Idiot bayside palms look down appalled
their leg-warmers pulled up high
around an electrified dentifrice of leaf hairs.

Beyond the knife-thin blades of the filtering blind
waves of new thought are marked at each driftline,
whitening spines of course readers in classical polity,
renaissance civics, undisturbed on the liberal shelves
above the generous white oak floors.

All the growth-enhanced wagons called Suburban
surf a conglomerate image ocean
past the speaking blankness of corporate ziggurats, next them
the structural nightmare of over-regulated strawberry fields
and the enormous investment in the bent backs of the peons
who pick in the wake of machines before the light begins to punish
but not soon enough for these race-class slaves
below whom are yet more tiers of unregistered souls
in the darkened sectors of south-central,
soils parching under asphalt and all the waters
for ever chemically locked in concrete.

Brought up short on the turn-out rest stop
by the show-cased missing children
next Colonel Saunders and the Rattler Warning,
bound down by the food-outlet tie-ins,
don't pass up the turn-out from the slow lane,

Opt for the corner-store stake-out
among threatening night-persons who riskily dance
with traffic at downtown intersections

Within the ring of fortress malls tinted uniform pink
leaching old trade, dumping volume good
forged in over-the-ocean-rim gulags

What is a child to see

Through the truthful purity of dust storms
that veil the punished freeway surfaces
and haze a future

Calling for the gift of childish rains.

Cara Alba Derelicta

I travelled under my movement name,
a margin mask flitting from face to face,
darkly modelling the usual heartwork
within her roofless houses and emptied livings.

We were hounds of the grey cloud mountain,
all through shrewd days and nights
forced beyond the forest burr and sought in quarter light
at the place where rock became fluid and the sky involved us.

Once as we ate secretly at the people's table,
breathing free from southern weight,
when our world-inheriting children
tied our hearts above our heads, then

A black iron thigh rolled slovenly
in mid-lochan, and sang noiselessly,
out-hearing our ears for some final word.

Was it for this we saw them ashen go down
to the bone-flecked peat, their names
called like Vilna unhearingly above you?

All day new water has worn the sky,
Cloudlight spread taught like a sacrament cloth.
And at the alarm fringe an ocean meniscus pushes
to our door lip: the spume line reaches
to the high dune system where we've lain
brushed out among marram, moonwort and fescue,
as the cold informed desire itself,
become burnished and proud.

Wheatears haunt this machair,
wind-drifted night migrants,
and a fall of goldcrest
for you and upon you.

March will bring spring ephemerals,
discretion birds who wing each heart
in their lightsomeness.

Ocean searches deep within herself for the water
that will clean these shore waters,
the damp slacks and intertidals who labour
under the large-scale redundancy of biological systems
now glossed by effluent. Like language which knows how to curse
she would cure herself. We've seen the old ones break
and become children again through a love and loss
                              they couldn't contain.
Unheard we call to you for the conversations broken-backed
                              mid-sentence and mid-sentiment,
the love only now become articulate.
When will life deliver us free of this failure for more?

New times call from between the sound of words:
for the sublimed vision of plenitude
occurs exactly within the condition
where it might be installed if only
we were simply to realize there is no earthly reason
why it should not be lived among us,
displacing some ungrasped element,
an ever smaller supplement which we have not possessed,
and called for, from the vantage of bliss.

Stands of pine harbour the frail spring ephemerals
as far tides drag and run beneath us, modelling deeply.
Inland call the thinly drifted tilts and folds
of a land surface scarified by geology and capital,
its carrs and tills a firm cantus
that clothes us in unreckonable rhythm.

Kissing bright and thousand lighted
in the burning rains, a stroke
and a seizure of lightsomeness
touches acid brown water to my eye-lips.
Remorse grains scratch at the film surface but
all our light is borne on the out-tide.

And I love you Alba then,
Outfacing dawn from the firestep.

The Plains of Sight

For the life and works of Gwen John
1876–1939

1989

A Working Life

She rose at the sill of each day
to combers of joy sweeping
the length of her straitened spine

The stress of her lines
nursed any body they would carry
in their cat's cradle
of a delicate tension

Their unconceived inconceivable natures
filling the inflected space of canvas

As grounds of being on which lease
might be taken, improbably calling
and freely given

She plays upon the key board
the tone row
of what is between us,
what at issue.

I am felt to be
like the slight ring

of a new coin
spun with deft fingers

in a room of complete silence

the arc of its turning sphere

curving with an inevitable grace
back to the previsionary hand

where it reassumes the geometry
of a still and quiet disk

A suffused window

a generous breakfast cup

unofficial flowers in a white jug

a chair that waits for no one:

what more could we want?

It is surely correct that
the sun does move

between the roofs of each street
bringing its shade

to a different place
with remarkable care

but is there anything to be said
from this as to progress
in the lives of people?

Nothing happened, she would claim, during the first twenty-seven years of her life, but *'Fifty years hence, I shall be remembered only as the Brother-of-Gwen'* trumpeted Augustus in 1946. And she wrote, *'It is because I cannot criticize the world I know, because I have not been able to criticize it, that it appears to have a value.'*

This world is a huge thing, and we are permeated by it, our bodies are only the most intimate category within its condition. And she is a painter of the figure of our lives, together with the forms in which we might patiently come to know each other.

And therefore she carried her affectivity like a garment, contemplation turned upon the material of the world, not so as to leave the case behind for something higher, but in order to transmute and have it rephrased by the full semantic ranges of love.

Her Subjects

'women, children, flowers, cats, a corner of some room, perhaps a curtain, sometimes a chair . . . paint no men'

The tops of trees, agitated with breeze
Two children against a pink background
Boy with a blank expression
Woman with a vacant smile
Young woman holding a black cat
Musing tabby
Cat cleaning itself
Wide-awake tortoise-shell cat
Ditto napping
Girl reading
Woman in rose
Corner of a room
Vine leaves in a white jug
An interior, highly dissolved, probably the painter's room

Colour Notes

'smoky corn & wild rose,
palid roses (three reds), nuts & nettles . . .
cyclamen & straw & earth'

'March 23 . . . elder berries & their yellow leaves
& pink campions & their cendre bleu green leaves'

'April . . . faded pansies on the sands at night'

'chimney cowls & autumn leaves,
garlic & its blue-black leaves
& faded primroses & straw'

'dewberries
ochres darkened with black turnings of the leaf'

There is a well-defined progress in the style of her work, which began carefully and securely in the minute exploitation of accumulated glazes, semi-transparent layerings of the paint, a method taught by Whistler and followed by her friend and contemporary, Ambrose McEvoy. Numbers of brushes were used, and in this particular school the full array of colour values was laid down on the palette before the canvas was even touched; then the masses of the figure were indicated by a tonal sculpture in grey, and *'when the palette presented as near a reproduction of the model and the background as the worker could obtain, the colour could be put down with a generous flowing brush'* (E. R. & J. Pennell, *The Life of Whistler*, 1908).

But at some period during 1910 the technique changes and becomes in effect a reversal of the first style: thickly impasted paint is used, the canvas is rarely touched more than once in applying the colour, and if errors are made then the whole portrait is begun again. The dark, virtually black shadows of the early style fade and vanish, as the tones of the whole surface become lighter, closer. Details evaporate before the inevitability of this progress and the compositional forms simplify and amass. Now the pictures are built from tesserae, mosaic-like fragments of chalky paint that are suspended in a quick-drying medium (which may even be petrol). During this phase the ground of the canvas itself is often left untouched, and shows through as the provisional plane on which the barely recorded figure of the sitter is hardly materialized.

She never knew of, and would almost certainly not have cared for, the work of a near-contemporary such as Egon Schiele, but there is silent complicity between the kinds of intense regard which they both addressed to the human figure. Schiele wrote in 1912 –

> *The picture must give out light of its own*
> *Bodies have their own light*
> *Which they exhaust in living*
>
> *They burn away*
> *They are unlighted*

Her later portraits completely inhabit the systematic transitions from light to dark, and it was for this kind of reason that Whistler must have felt that there was no character in her figures, only a massively developed sense of tone. This conveys an achieved impersonality, one of the values so intensively sought after during the period of European high Modernism (with which she had nothing to do). This essentializing of the figure without dwelling on the local eccentricity of the individual was a version of the classicist's desire to be effaced, or unfaced, and remain withdrawn behind the picture's plane of reference. The figures are bound to their articulation by a complete evenness of attention, and their greyness makes them appear to have been dusted by a light fall of volcanic ash.

In obsessively repeating the same motif through a number of hardly perceptible variations, she could arrive at a kind of perfection. She recorded the progress of light as it made its way between and across (and then also through) the objects of her room, and as it elicited the natures of her models. She never signed or dated any work. But was she simply dissolving the world under this play of illumination? And would this then be the most damaging (the most inhuman) formalism of all? To hope to paint, not so much any of the objects or persons obscurely presented in the canvas, but simply the falling of the light itself, as it abolished the surfaces on which it lay? Yet her women in grey remain formidably present, they seem to be gathered about their own hands which rest in their laps, cupped and self-addressed, or crossed and stowed, simultaneously prompt and renounced.

The final phase of her work was given exclusively to gouaches and water colour, as she committed herself to the veiling and blinding of flattened fields of completely suffused colour which allowed no chance of correction. For these she used Japanese papers because *'coulours* [sic] *don't run into each other. The paper absorbs the colour with each touch of the brush so that it is final, there is no retouching.'*

Ways of Working and Notes to Self

'Rule One: the drawing is the discord'

'Method of Observation: 1 the strangeness – 2 colour – 3 tones – 4 form'

'The Making of the Portrait: 1 the strange form – 2 the pose and proportions – 3 the atmosphere & notes – 4 the finding of the forms: the sphere, the hair, the forehead, the cheek, the eye, the nose, the mouth, the neck, the chin, the torse – 5 blobbing – 6 the sculpting with the hands'

She wrote: 'I am patient and receuillé [collected] in some degree
BUT I DON'T WANT TO SEE ANY ENGLISH PICTURES EVER AGAIN'

'The time I give to it, waiting, attending, desiring'

From a letter of August 1936: 'A cat or a man,
it's the same thing – an affair of volumes'

'Today the sky is low, everything is grey and covered with mist –
it is a good day to paint – But I think of people'

And towards the end, she could write – 'We have not much
to do with people, perhaps nothing directly'

She was described – 'unaffected, concentrated, direct, withdrawn,
still the same strange reserved creature . . . impitoyable'
that is, ruthless, merciless, unrelenting.

If you are unsympathetic to her images, you will say that they are insipid, as did the American reviewer for *TIME* magazine, visiting the 1946 retrospective exhibition:

'Many of the paintings look as if they had faded in the sun . . . They are as limited and dim as reflections in a cup of cold tea.'

But the reviewer for the London *Times* entered into the spirit of the work more accurately:

'The colours are faint . . . Those who expect painting to provide a knock-out blow will be disappointed . . . There are none of the qualities to be found here that attract strong men to the prize ring.'

From a pieran distance

The stars lease heartsblood

             upon you

And coldly but deeply a stellar truth

             rains on you

At your word the heart falls open

             like an over-read book:

And who is the injured, who the adored?

These Portraits

They give an absolute attention

They offer no vicious possession of their subject

They express no sentimentality, desire, or hatred for what they show

Their opened passivity is a most complete image of our endurance

Only in this sense might they be called religious

Through a gravity which makes us fall toward their heights

Eight Lines

The life with which you have just woken now begins to fit more loosely,

A winter coat suddenly become inappropriate.

It is bright morning again, and even today water flows smoothly

From the tap. See, touch it, upon your inner wrist:

Soon our collective days will begin to widen, gape – step carefully

So as not to fall between them, into the punishing noise

Which lies waiting at the heart of spring silence.

There is a terror in thresholds; here is the year's door.

As if from the Russian

1986

Rus, Rus

Who calls through the birds, winged items
drifting down the film frame,

Plumage storm, narrative of bitter pennies
as if snow were to fall within our house?

The stars draw up and
I am sorry to have left them
so far away:

Here below our vacant chairs settle
around the firmly waiting table:

Beyond the frost-inscribed pane
is the earth in which our parents sleep

And we lie upon it like children
who know a thing or perhaps two.

Great unknown birds crash above

Great unknown birds crash above
and below the ice
there is fire.

Maybe I'll go live with the Ultras,
take on a protective colouring
and hide out north of the river
where you can be cooled by the insistent storm
of observing helicopter blades
during those burning days of black terror.

Since the turn of the century
the bourgeoisie has everywhere known and felt
that it deserved to die

And they embrace 'the will of god'
which is no more than
the asylum of ignorance.

It is a murmur that strikes across my heart
like cold breeze
on a deep old lake

This question of a crime
whose scale reaches exactly
to all meaning.

Wren-sharp, wren-shy

Wren-sharp, wren-shy
the hedge rows
and mile upon mile

Of elm death:
massed starling crowds
twist within

Like aerial regiments
a granular stream
the creaturely curl

Of bird on bird
where each bird
flies alone and
each bird flies

Together

A cold lightning

A cold lightning
tears the sky silk

Truth is overnamed
and long since fell
below the speech levels
of our world's inaudible
silence

En Route

Summerless
when the stars were ploughed
into strict regimen

and close by the emptied word

safety howled at a short rein

Kardiotissa

Fresh old roses climbed high among apple boughs:
paired cherries fell and clung like sins to lower branches.

The creature perhaps a bird sang
in fury
within the window depth as
inner temperatures cool
to ice blue.

The logic was such that
we first had to burn furniture,
then floorboards and skirting, finally the books,
following a strict order of priorities
until only the police-proof invisible editions remained
hidden within coat linings or beneath the skin,

And you were a prisoner with so little in the world
that you dreamt ecstatically of evangelists flying
like a band of nine swifts scything air
above Vilnius, Odessa, Tbilisi.

Selections of children floated down river,
huddled within a night tent, singing their songs,
and the light of ten thousand refugee camp dawns
machine-stitched infinite severities above them.

Tsaritsyn

My index makes a night touch
of the light wine to your nape

And you arch against it
your face towards all that is not to be seen.

It is within the ever-closing distance
of these never-meeting hands
that almost everything must be said.

Nothing is truly antagonistic –
in plurality we pass
through reactionary dark,

Your inner line turning me
through five dimensions
where all fierce distance is white.

Elousa

*To admit
is not to enter, the door is not an ikon.*

Within the golden panels that abolish colour
into our living room
you call down the Baptist and selected angels.

Gold is your background even as
gold is nowhere in the spectrum
of the world

and the night sky slides away
like a plate of devalued coin.

Sung before Sunrise

Sometimes it feels as if the blood withdraws
from my surfaces, and it may be that
the only way to proceed
is to lean more severely into the wind

And set shoulder to our relation
as if I was changing a tractor tyre
under hard rains of an endless taiga –

But let us drink tomorrow's wine:
weightless your arm above me,
                              its emptied wrist,
untensioned and proximate like the least profile
which in moving yields
a face flowering in absolute value –

Is there no pity, sitting in the clouds?
As the inner line of crisis moves across your terrain
and introjects to deep unknown centres
this must be the time to register
the world's hard lines, the world's starvation
within our thin words as they close about our objectless unease.

It may be that
from tomorrow's wine we will draw strength
to negotiate the cash-filled streets
and all their forms of human incompletion,

We, who never fed at ease upon the surfaces
but took the curving truth
with brimming hands
from each warm and blooded heart.

Stem Glass, Cutting Garden

Innerly the chorus at dawn sings
Pale birds and an iron light
Hanging above fraught headland

While a last star curvets
Over the high forehead of bright cloud
And our song cuts inward

Making birdspace below the heartline
Fluent and running dayspring
For this earth is on high

Clearly held by no thing
As the skyshield now shines before day's breast
Burnished with a deep and heavenly care

The grain of your flesh begins here
At edge of my finger tips
And the folds of attraction fall from your hips

Raking the ashen heart to intelligible flame
A condition in the world
Like the tension of dance

Where our musics are the stem glass
Of this relation
Shot through by the broken behaviours

Of great light

White Love, White Ship

This late afternoon August sun
rakes across all surfaces, making pointed comparisons:
who treats the fields so algebraically?

When the waters had frozen in waves,
and this Summer's lilies were no more
than a pale intention under ground,
a comet burned briefly, a night sun
in the lowest aspect of sky –
many of us hoped to pierce
the city glow, ride its tail.

And it has been an eloquent season
of white long-sided skirts
but now the present becomes insubstantial
as the field of vision fills
with brightly coloured romper suits.
By day and by night
in the silence of the pedestrianized mall
money continues to ooze
from an acid green hole set firm
in the wall.
All qualities are depthless as the mirror-lined shop called 'YOU',
a vacancy through which the future endlessly rushes
to become the pasts which are so desperately embraced.

Swimmer, take your mark!
The brisk waters of September lie before you,
quilting the dark and the light.
Leaves cast by trees applaud your sport,
and at the closing of our poem
I ask you all a question:
was it for this that Lenin died
whispering 'Americanize yourselves'?

Strong Lines Recessional Numbers

1980

Be submissive to the authorities!   George Grosz

It is acceptable to punch another man on the nose in the boxing ring (place stimulus) but not the referee (person stimulus) or a man you meet at work (person and place stimulus). It is acceptable to shout at your children (person stimulus) or at a footballer when in a football crowd (place stimulus) but not to shout at your boss (person stimulus) or a policeman (person stimulus).

From 'The Trainee Manual', page 8, on 'Stimulus Control', in *Education of the Developmentally Young: The Behaviour Modification Approach*, University of Manchester, (1978).

Dern

That summer of soulful nineteenth-century starlettes
muffled in emotional cloak, they gazed from the hoardings
as you rushed me into doorways
to shelter us from turbulence of the streets,

The blood of our shared day giving on to
elf nights that rose like smoke of incense
in a breezeless room, straight and exalted
as lady birch, when we would divide and burn

In many places, our talk the lost messages
of a re-entrant ship, silenced by the glow
of planet embrace, falling, in love with earth,
words abolished at the heat frontier

Of space and world, into this yearless time
of hats and coats that feel the lack
of bodies about which to be draped

The time of the heart's priorities
this time of national unity
and newscasters with thinly decorated chests
the time of no-go, time of the watching brief
the time of women with blackened eyes who walk the streets
as if by accident, the time of bit jobs
the bookless time, the time of typical girls,
time of the sundial lost in snow

The time of 'What need one?'

Time of 24 police officers equal one Serial
time of rough trade, of wording it late
under strip neon in the night school,
the time of billiard-hall days and space-invaded nights
this time of quadruple double glazing, if you can afford it

These wolf years, eaten of poets
times of the technico-emotive problem

and of tying and loosing, time of Saturday Cash Point angst,
the time of light from neither sun nor moon

Time of the alert objects
standing about the full cup of History
they gently dip their cursory fingers
and ride the sweeping curve of now

when the world is spoken by human time

as a glass given shape by its water.

Night and its Dour Prestigia

NIGHT and its dour prestigia
call down upon the world

As muezzin for the faithless
who unregretting do not look back

NIGHT your music falls on them
like a cope of silence

NIGHT the moon burns through you
& takes me the other side

NIGHT all dreams turn in you
& scent the day thereafter

NIGHT the dark is material
and no simple privation

NIGHT your kiss to earth
heals the eye of each daisy

And Cold Foot burns twigs
under the blanket edge of day

As Night Quiet creeps
in the fire surcingle

Purrs within the ashes and
hushes the riven blood of evening

The eyes of watching Naturalists
eat from your hands, Night,

Gorged on a bran of disquiet
from the dead mills of observation

The cone of your lightless sight
arcs into the deeper Night of stealth

where I was to write a cheque for the unknown girl
whose name arranged itself indifferently under the pen:

Goat suckers continued to sing as the dream insisted
'Wolverine de Lamborghetta' in a far-back voice.

My clerkly heart banked the imperfect note
across love's semi-permeable membrane.

The home service filled my ears and not a room
was untaken by shroud makers.

To a sequence of moons the pain grew
while men with time to read lectured women

Only with time to listen: all their great talk
was a dereliction of what might been said

as unmarked pages crossed the stellar space
between them without these most telling formulae:

Deeply Programmed in the Main of Light

This was a singing of the travels.

They went by Shade Way
across barren high ground
& the deserted barn,
flapping their palms upon bland plates
of gross water plant
like salvers under the moon:

And Black Shuck waits at
the trust house carrefour:
— young men on walking tours & reading parties
— entire coach contents of the mystery trip
— each travelling rep & his coat hanger
— artics of sea-worn consumer durables
& black shod duos of combination lovers

Have vanisht to line his snapping maw
subject of reportage on the vicinity hospital network.

By the doorstep of my feelings
& the jamb of my heart
I sat me down, Babylon,
or rather Littleport

& listened to the slight forces
that allow the inner workings
to be heard.

We took firehooks from the mainstreet,
turning in the direction
of the orchestrated blaze
as our children

Ask for 'Work' for breakfast.
This licit world & its rotten peculation
parrots SIC & NON
and we walk the unadopted road

This is no way to go on:

In the Sharp Mode of Failure

Instant fires run through occulting light
and shall we not tend to perfection?

Not wanting either to die or to live
but both simultaneously ask me no more
what kind of question is it
that bites off its own mark
destroyed at both ends of the scale

As the golden seed of all
furrows through its sky
and fiery youths who lick
their sweat from each other's spine

Disrobe to face
the folds of warmth
their upper legs stained
in smoke from battles

Far distant in the provincial universe
fronded with power
their faces blanched by long years
under the neon ceilings of integrated offices

But with warm combs of hand-finished ivory
they perfect the falls of hair
for their most-loved warrior
and grow younger
admiring these plaited weirs
reflected by polished weapon edges

In coats of eyes and tongues they walk
the running deep
like ones hidden in strong love
of the people

They bear proud the neck bites
of experience

Moon-soled within the social world
with how sad steps

Their modest glory starts through
the wet sands
about their feet
the ocean moves in its convenient channels

And everyone shortens their dreams
as pillars of air weave and thread
their arms above the shores of world
dealing level and walking the edge

With no point they descant heedlessly
intent sharp and cold as the claw
of an arctic lion
like a three-horned flame

Of irreproachable feeling
the equal women dance within the pale
fretted with modern pain
and golden leather garments

The black cherries of their eyes
would move beyond the fences
of their ornate and painted fingers
sweep the audience of firesome youths
to cash the sexual bargain
struck in the streets

Where folding money crisp & valueless
calls the tune, that one tune
among dark and equal chaos
such full-blooded sport

The beast from the land
comes over red event horizon
steel eyelids snapping

in the arc of crisis
where no writ runs

Bluetooth Wartooth and Sawtooth
jockey for strategic depth
around gull paths to spring
their mawsome traps

The wavebands join together
for announcements of a common interest
as international flights shut down
I find historical meaning in dust of my turnups

And under your horse-mired mask
delicately starving
you wrap the great coat

Of feminine negation
more closely about the denied core
of what you might be

One of the strangely phrased children
the pre-dead of consumer life
who walk planetary slopes

& hear with razor clarity
the fires of class difference

All-Niter

after a night of love

stock market sentiment takes a dive
wise up to this
the old bag of threadbare street
says we are living beyond our means

after a night of love

with Maggie who chose to tell us
how to run our lives
out of purest idealism & absolutely no
self-interest involved

after a night of love

the Queen speaks to the heart of
every christian christmas dinner
legitimizing her familial hegemony

after a night of love

the dopes who jack off on obscurity
return to their padded choir stalls
& stay inside careers founded
on deconstruction

after a night of love

the impurities of language
float to the surface
and the only metaphysical condition to be in
is danger

after a night of love

and soups various the individuals of principle
resign on the spot

the engine & its gallant crew
vanish inside the fireball

after a night of love

hospitals bleed to death
daddy's arms are not strong enough
and mummy's love evaporates like
a ruptured gaz cylinder

after a night of love

houses cease to be homes
and all roads lead to the cemetery
abyssal lethality strikes
the street of 1000 window stylers

after a night of love

bitter as the evening class
on 'love in English literature'
through the pairing winter nights
do not grieve

after a night of love

that the battle is reduced
to innumerable local skirmishes
for the struggle becomes pandemic
descends to within your every cell

after a night of love

and is the classic terrorist structure
with unity of purpose unknown
beyond the gathered three or four
drawing a bead

after a night of love

with an utterly desperate aim
on the impossible future
one foot already
in the next street

after a night of love

The Windshield Glarestrip Legends

1979

The bi-metal strip cuts in and out

It is the night workers' hours
invert
and between the railway tracks
the gangers in their fluorescent tabards
lift and wrench against the resistant lines
restricted to their narrowest strip
of harboured safety, the gang boss
looking to and fro for the curving arrival
of mixed goods and passenger trains

As his men earn their money
by work schematically dangerous
in these most arduous margins
of a restriction we can only theoretically know

As the year declines . . .

As the year declines into the black box
of the freezer
the flight recorder and all the leaves
fall from the sky
sought by contrary powers

The smile loosens on your face
preprandial sun
working up some emotion
the smile drifts into asparagus-tipped middle distance

It is a difficult thing I have to tell you I
have come to the point where I canot see my
way no more. Our life together has been a
fictitious lie. I canot stand you hanging
around my bum no longer.
Please excuse the
Writing.

The ice maidens dance worried

The ice maidens dance worried
not possessing their steps
looking about them for the anxiety
they have not yet left behind.

It comes at them between down beats.
The rudies are never more present
than now, musically
lifted into themselves.

O my northern soul
stript to the waist
turn on the balls of your feet
to fill this hall with your pleats.

Scrupulously indifferent

Scrupulously indifferent
the sun flowers turn back
their heads on flexing stems
to a moon
snagged on the plane trees
a silvered boss
that has nothing to do with us

and I drink from your impartial distances

tendered

So light are our hands
not yet inimical

for the rounding fruit of again
self-offering, offered

as we kiss the black rose
of midnight between us

The sun and the moon pour down

The sun and the moon pour down
the silence like milk
holding our attention
by not completing its pause

Your spine curves with all its kind
to the heavens
and we burn our selves
more deeply on the other

From deep within the heavens
the love pours down
to deep within the breast
stroked by this breeze upon you

It is clear you call down

It is clear you call down
a terrible value
fiercer than heat of the sun

A hand may spread out
and all of the sky will stream
between tendered fingers

The heart's solar wind
blackening
to a fiery rose

black-dyed herds of punks

black-dyed herds of punks
flow and recoil upon the northern line
children of nothing
while the lesbian estate
turns in perfection
upon the circle line
under the ground
the good gay guys
are still looking
for the way out of
the riff stroking
our expected gratification
behind and between the bars
we stop and start
looking for some way out
of circular desire

please come and go with me

furtive predations

furtive predations
on the body of love

the poems get thinner
as perception levels out

peaks at its tolerance
a strategic horizon

beyond which convention
lies burning in a reed hut

with villagers, community
let gone for nothing

And the Moon's franchise contracts

And the Moon's franchise contracts
in course of each month.
She is Madonna of the Sign
shedding ikon-cold kisses.
Terrible victories have been won
in her name.

Time was when we were happy
even for hours together.
No-one will now ever know why
as the steel circlet cools
around the throat of our joy.

Feast yourself *he said*

Feast yourself he said
in the falling woods
as the year closed in.
Reaching for the black
berries on the agonized twig

My wing is silent he said
like an owl in the night,
not to be heard

The last of the sun
shoots an ochre bolt

Venetian words

Slicks and rips ran eel-fast
beneath the lagoon, hammer-beaten
by an early rain burst:

In the evening we stalked fire flies
that might have been moving
within the constellated dark
of cypress trees,

Beyond which true light struck
like a night-long infection
burning among storm clouds.

Moonlight Becomes You But I Prefer the Sun

A remarkable fact of the universe
in terms of the standard big bang theory
is the evenness of all phenomena.
Here under these battles of light
the beer is cloudy but the night is clear
and the sun and the vein of the world fight it out.

Within the heart's unguarded fire
death is an admission of failure,
an after-loss in the under-croft
within the tracts of late time.

Paired drunks cling about bottles
which emptied
they fastidiously abandon
in unobtrusive corners of the cityscape

And their kisses become birds
between the up-turned stars of the lake.

More than ourselves

Love wielding itself in gestures of power,
power extending itself with claims of love,
the body politic, the body, torn by the privacy of love.

The stars are indeed marvellous
I see straight to your root
and smile with absolute welcome
cracking your codes, reader,
you have no secrets here
being under the contradictions most directly.

I make love to you in all those words
which are the first and last place to which we come.

Walking through the world

Who looks out of this face and eyes today
who walks with these legs
on the dust of this earth
who but the not to be escaped?

Across your shallows some breeze pertains
and the colour of the ocean
changes more deeply

I enter that specific blankness
which offers less than nothing
the book is upside down
the Leonids rise over the British Isles
and Mars is an evening star
lost in the sunset glow

The smallest hours of nightless sleep
wait at the bar of access
when closing my eyes I'd seal you
into my conception
that dark inescapably mine
of which I tire
unless I gain
the tender inward curve
of you

Three Qasídas
translated with Walid Abdul-Hamid

Impossible Traces: Translating the *Sayfiyat* of al-Mutanabbí
(304–354 AH, 915–965 CE)

Travelling from Iran to Iraq in 354 Anno Hegirae (965 CE) Abu Tayyib
Ahmad ibn al-Husain al-Mutanabbí was attacked by bandits at Dayr
al-'Aqul near Baghdad. His first impulse was to escape, but one of his
servants protested, 'Master, didn't you say in your *Sayfiyat*, "Horses, night
and the desert know me, and the sword, spear, paper and pen"'? Perhaps
stung by this quotation of his own most famous line against himself, the
poet turned to fight, but was killed in the encounter (Irwin, 1999: 221).
So ended the life of al-Mutanabbí, considered by many to be the greatest
classical Arab poet. One hundred years after al-Mutanabbí's murder, Abu
Ala al-Maari, poet and critic, wrote that he sometimes felt the desire to
alter the occasional word in al-Mutanabbí's verses, but he never managed
to improve on the original (Nicholson 1930: 308). It's probably the case
that no other pre- or post-Islamic poet has been the object of so much
commentary and criticism as al-Mutanabbí. His audacious spirit is evident
from his name, which means 'The Would-Be Prophet'; in his early 20s he
had tried to create a new religious movement among the Syrian Bedouin.

The poems translated here are taken from al-Mutanabbí's *Sayfiyat*, a
series of praise-poems addressed to prince Ali Sayf al-Dawla al-Hamdanid
(c. 327–346 AH, 948–957 CE), the emir of a small state situated in what is
now Syria. Sayf al-Dawla was a cultured, charismatic leader who for a
time managed to resist the incursions of the Byzantine empire during a
period when the rest of the Arab world was dominated by corrupt and
ineffectual leaders (Kennedy 1986: 275–87). Al-Mutanabbí spent nine years
under the patronage of Sayf al-Dawla and wrote over 12,000 lines of
praise poetry for the prince. The *Sayfiyat* – 'poems for Sayf' – consists
of eighty qasídas, or odes, and throughout these poems – which, taken
as a sequence, might be described as the first epic in Arabic poetry – al-
Mutanabbí persistently plays on the meaning of Sayf al-Dawla's name,
'Sword of the State'. According to Taha Husain, an influential twentieth-
century Egyptian critic, these poems are not only al-Mutanabbí's finest
work, but they are some of the most striking poetry written in Arabic
(Husain 1937: 169, and Gomez 1941). In spite of this status in Arabic
literary culture, very few of these odes have been translated into English.
The qasídas of the *Sayfiyat* focus on praise of Sayf al-Dawla, extolling
his pure Arab lineage, his generosity and bravery, but they also cover a

great range of registers and subjects, due partly to the sophistication of Sayf al-Dawla's court culture, and partly to the variety of themes which al-Mutanabbí introduced. There are for example 'hidden' love poems addressed to Khawla, the emir's sister, who could never have been directly addressed by a mere poet. However alien they may seem to us now, these conventions of the Arabic encomium share striking similarities with the praise-poetry traditions and warrior society ethos of Celtic and early modern Britain (compare Conran 1967).

Why do we read so little classical Arabic poetry in English translation? For that matter, why do we read so little Arabic literature of any sort? It's partly the difficulty of transposing anything of the compelling music and cultural resonance of poems in Arabic, but also, surely, for historical reasons, including an unwillingness to engage with the 'otherness' of Arabic and Islamic cultures. Al-Mutanabbí's poetry can be found in English translation in specialist academic journals and monographs (Arberry 1967, Hamori 1992, Sperl and Shackle 1996) but it rarely reaches a wider English readership.

We have made these versions in two stages: first from Arabic to English by Walid Abdul-Hamid, and then via conversation and 'indirect' translation with Nigel Wheale (for which see Clive Wilmer 2000). In a qasída the number of verses ('abyát') may vary from twenty to over a hundred. Each 'bayt' is divided into two parts or 'misrá': 'sadr', the chest, and 'ajiz', the hip. In the first verse each half shares the same end-rhyme, which is then repeated once in every following verse. Rhymes are more easily come by in Arabic than in English, because of the nature of word formation, but even so this mono-rhyming discipline is extraordinarily demanding, and, we found, impossible to reproduce. Metrical forms in the qasída are also highly structured, a music not available to English. We have added verse paragraph divisions to indicate changes of subject in the qasída because these transitions can often seem abrupt, as it was a part of the poet's skill to persuade his audience to follow his flights of association between topics. We hope that new readers may gain some sense of al-Mutanabbí's qualities through our distant versions of his song.

Primary text
Al-Mutanabbí, Abu 'l-Tayyib (1861) *Diwan, with commentary by al-Wahidi* (464 AH/1075 CE), ed. F. Dieterici, Berlin.
— *Diwan* (1964) with commentary, ed. Nasif [and Ibrahim] al-Yazjii, Beirut, Dar Sadir.

References

Arberry, A. J. (1967) *Poems of Al-Mutanabbi. A Selection with Introduction, Translations and Notes*, Cambridge University Press.

Conran, Anthony, in association with J. E. Caerwyn Williams (1967) translating Gruffudd ab yr Ynad Coch's 'Lament for Llywelyn the Last' (c. 1282 CE), pp. 128–131, 'the greatest poem, probably, in the Welsh language' (p. 41) in *The Penguin Book of Welsh Verse*, Harmondsworth, Penguin.

Gomez, Emilio Garcia (1941) *Mutanabbi. El Mayor Poeta de los Arabes (915–965)*, Madrid, Ediciones Escorial.

Hamori, Andras (1992) *The Composition of Mutanabbi's Panegrics to Sayf al-Dawla*, Leiden, Brill.

Husain, Taha (n.d., [1936]) *Maa al-Mutanabbi* [*With The Mutanabbi*], Cairo, Dar Al Maarif.

Irwin, Robert (1999) *Night and Horses and the Desert. An Anthology of Classical Arabic Literature*, Harmondsworth, The Penguin Press.

Kennedy, Hugh (1986) *The Prophet and the Age of the Caliphates. The Islamic Near East from the Sixth to the Eleventh Century*, Harlow, Pearson Education.

Nicholson, R. A. (1930, 1993) *A Literary History of the Arabs*, Richmond, Curzon Press.

Sperl, S. and C. Shackle (eds) (1996) 'Qasida Poetry in Islamic Asia and Africa', *Studies in Arabic Literature XX*.

Wilmer, Clive (2000) 'Two modes of translation: the direct and indirect', *PN Review 132*.

He Said to His Prince and Patron Sayf al-Dawla

There was a time when shame stopped my tears,
    But now grief opens my heart,
Each bone screaming
    Within the flesh, every vein tearful.
The beauty of this white gazelle
    Equals the despair she feeds in me.
She was revealed, but veiled with the paleness of leaving,
    It masked the red and the white of her presence,
 As if tears coursed down her face,
    Gold overlaid with a stream of pearl.
She parted three falls of hair
    On that night, she tressed four nights together.
She returned the night's sun in her face,
    Slaying me with two lights in one.
The comb-line in her hair delights perfume's heart.
    The hearts of iron and leather helmets are struck with sorrow
Comparing themselves, shielding the heads of warriors,
    To her head's veil, they envy that cloth its place.
No woman graces rubies like her,
    No man graces more the beauty of his sword's hilt.
May the time of our courting return and her camp be watered,
    Endless showers, moist as the memory of our courtship.
A rain-burst breaks, firing the air, turning the desert
    To sea, parched dunes made over to drenched plain.

                 •

The dear one is as handsome as if beauty had chosen him,
    Or the share-giver unfairly favoured him.
The spears of Khatt protect him from capture
    But take prisoners for him from the strongest tribes.
His furthest screen is the dust of warriors' horses,
    Smoke of incense that surrounds him the closest.
    And better than all the waters of youth
    Is the rain-promising lightning I see within this tent.

The meadows upon these awnings are watered by no cloud.
    No doves sing in the branches of these trees.
Over cloths patterned on both sides weave
    Pearl strings never pierced by the jeweller.
Here is the peaceable creaturely kingdom,
    Where hunting beasts are at war and peace.
When the breeze stirs they move
    Horses high-step in parade, lions set out to hunt.
The image of the Byzantine crown performs submission
    To his dawn-white face crowned only by a turban.
The lips of kings kiss his carpet,
    His sleeve and hand too great for intimacy.
All stand for him whose fires cure all,
    Whose brand is burned into every hero's face.

•

O thou the most just of all – though not to me –
    In you is the quarrel, you both judge and jury.
I appeal to your searching glance
    Not to mistake my swollen limbs for prosperity.
What use is sight to any living being
    If he cannot tell apart the shades of light and dark?
I whose poetry could make the blind see,
    Whose words brought hearing to the deaf.
I sleep, eyes well sealed, no longer chasing metaphors,
    While everyone else is awake, disputing my meaning.
Horses, night and the desert know me,
    And the sword, spear, paper and pen.
I ran with wild beasts alone among dunes,
    Astounding the rocks and the hills.
O thou whom we find difficult to leave,
    After you everything will be as nothing.

•

You wearied the dawn light with your raiding,
    You wearied the night dark with your armed bands,
You wearied spears with chest-breaching heart-blows,

You wearied the blade-wielded Indian steel,
You, clouded with eagles, beneath whom the marching clouds,
Watering fierce raptors with white swords.

•

Sayf al-Dawla ordered his army to a difficult task
Which greater forces had never achieved.
He asks men to possess what his soul possesses,
A task beyond the lion-hearted.
Yet the best of birds would sacrifice their lives for his swords,
The desert eagles, young and old,
Would not go hungry if they were created without talons
Thanks to his swords and those who grip them.
He razed red Hadath, while clashing spears
And the wave of deaths collided all around
As if the worst madness dwelt there.
The bodies of the dead were like charms upon it,
A refugee to time that had been taken and which you brought back,
Returned to religion with spears in spite of time.
Nights relinquish whatever you take from them.
They have to return whatever they take from you.
When you utter the verb of command
It is fulfilled even before the accent is inked down.
You stood and there was no doubting Death where you stood
As if you were at the eyelid of Death as he slept.
Heroes pass you injured and defeated
And your face shines and your lips smile.
You surpassed the height of courage and reason,
Men said you could know the unknown.
You have folded their wings back on to their heart,
A folding that destroys both plume and under-feathers.
Victory was absent as blows struck heads,
Triumph delivered when they cleaved the upper chest.
You spurned spears and threw them away,
The sword disdaining the lance.
Whoever wants great conquest will need
As his key your swords white, sharp and light.

You threw your enemy over the steep mount of Ohidab
    As if you scattered a confetti of bride money.
You rode up among the highest nests,
    You created food for the scavenging young.
The eaglets thought you had visited them
    With their mothers and not with strong steeds.
If horses lost footing you forced them to crawl on their bellies
    As snakes crawl on the ground.
O thou sword that is never sheathed
    There is no doubting its strength, no protection from it.

•

Though we know the road, we demanded in Najd,
    How long will we be on the way?
When gardens welcomed us we answered
    Aleppo is our aim, you merely the route.
You the pasture for our horses and camels,
    Our horse-speed the passage to Aleppo.
I had deserted him, flying to furthest east and west,
    Yet his bounty goes before me wherever I turn
And is with me whichever way I take;
    In every journey I make he underwrites me.
No one but thou Ali is a hero
    Whose sword is unsheathed for high honour.
How could Iraq and Egypt not feel safe,
    When your horses and squadrons shield them?
If you moved a fraction from the path of the enemy
    Their horses would bind the date palm with the date plum,
Those guarded by your defence
    Would know the depths of their submission to you.
Mere men have given up trying to follow you,
    It is spears and blades that now deliver your aim.

•

He who serves death in his company
    Sets himself apart from those who merely serve wine.
Distance has robbed me of the intimacy of your gift-giving,

My pasture is green but my body is wasting.
Even if I died into the life where other gifts are granted,
  Your gifts would surely follow me.
I do not care, so long as the binding ropes of night spare you,
  Whoever else is cut down in their strength and sanity.

This is a composite qasída where we have combined passages from several praise-poems to Sayf al-Dawla. The opening 'nasib' is the conventional address to a beloved, in this case Khawla, Sayf al-Dawla's sister, from the poem to Abdul Al Wahid Ibn Abas Ibn Abi Al Asbassba al-Katib. This is followed by: the elegy to Khawla from *Sayfiyat* 79; 'The dear one ' from the praise-poem to Sayf al-Dawla, *Sayfiyat* 1; 'O thou most just of all', *Sayfiyat* 35; 'Sayf al-Dawla ordered', *Sayfiyat* 67; 'Though we know the road', *Sayfiyat* 80. Two lines in the translation represent one line in the original. Here is Al-Mutanabbí's most celebrated line, 'Horses, night and the desert . . .', line 29 in this translation:

أَلْخَيْلُ واللَّيْلُ والبَيداءُ تَعرِفُني
والسَّيفُ والرُمحُ والقِرطاسُ والقَلَمُ

And he spoke, lamenting the death of Sayf al-Dawla's mother, consoling him for her loss in the year 337

We may gather the finest swords and spears
> But death kills us without struggle.
We may keep swift horses close at hand
> But they will not save us from the raids of time.
From antiquity people have loved life
> But there is no way to court and win its favours.
Your share in life from your beloved
> Is no more than your share in sleep from a dream.
Decades have afflicted me with troubles,
> My heart is covered over with a thick hide of arrow heads.
When the next shaft strikes my heart
> The blade shatters as if against another blade.
Time became more merciful when I ceased to care
> Because caring could not protect me.

·

This poem is the first elegy
> For the first death of such majesty,
As if death had never struck before
> Or never passed through any consciousness.
May Allah our Creator shroud with mercy
> Her face already wrapped in beauty.
O you now shielded with dust,
> Your shield before death was nobility.
O you now wrapped in the womb of earth,
> Your memory is reborn as you decay.
It consoles our soul that you died a death
> Desired by both the quick and the dead
And you departed without a single sad day
> On which a soul might have wished to die.

·

A canopy of glory stood high above you
        And the reign of your son Ali was perfected.
May generous rains bless your resting place
        Just as your hands showered gifts with bounty,
An earth-bruising rain with the strength
        Of horses as they race to their feed.
After your death I sought you in every glory,
        Because I know no glory not granted by you.
A beggar will pass by your grave and cry
        And his weeping prevents his begging.
You would not need to have been asked
        If you were able to perform the act.
Have you in death forgotten your giving,
        Since I who received can never forget?

                              •

You have descended against our wishes to a place
        Where you are far from Noama and Shimal,
        [Breezes of the south and the north,]
Veiled from the scent of Khozama,
        Denied the mild dew of dawn,
In a house where every dweller is homeless,
        A stranger in that land and rootless,
Untainted like the waters of rain in which
        A secret is locked and whose speech is truthful.

                              •

She was treated by a physician of ailments
        And her son is physician of glory:
If he hears of disease at the border
        He prescribes a medicine of sharp spears.
For she is not like any woman
        To whom the grave grants chastity,
During whose funeral the market traded,
        Whose farewell was just the shaking of dust from sandals.

                              •

Princes walked around her barefoot
>As if hard stones were soft ostrich feathers.
For her the hidden women appeared unveiled,
>Scentless, dark-staining their faces.
The catastrophe befell them suddenly,
>Tears of true sadness diluting their tears of petulance.
If all women compared to this lost one
>Then women must be preferred to men.
The Sun suffers no dishonour because of its feminine name,
>No more does the masculine name of the Moon.

•

The worst thing in this death is finding
>The one we lost had no equal before death.
We bury each other, those who come after
>Now walking on the bodies of their ancestors.
The kohl of eyes once passionately kissed
>Is now mixed with pebbles and sand.
The eye is sealed that was unblinking in danger.
>He who feared wasting is now utterly decayed.

•

Thou Sayf al-Dawla seek help in patience,
>Your patience that is sought by mountains.
You teach people the way of endurance
>And how to ford death in the heat of battle.
Time's affairs ebb and flow
>But your bearing stands unchanged.
May the ocean of your giving never weaken
>In treating the poor out-caste.
I see you among those seen as kings,
>The keen edge among dull blades,
Exceeding mankind, though you are one of them,
>Thou, musk from the blood of gazelle.

Zuhair, an Arabic Poet of Peace

Zuhair Ibn Abi Salma (520–610 CE) is one of the most celebrated poets of the Jahiliyya, as the period of pre-Islamic Arabic culture is known. His qasída or ode translated here is one of the seven poems (ten in some versions) described as the 'Mu'allaqat' or 'suspended' poems. It is not clear why they are remembered in this way, but one tradition records that they were draped on the sides of the shrine of the Qaaba in Mecca, written in golden letters on linen hangings. They are therefore also remembered as 'the golden odes' and have influenced poetry written in Arabic ever since, as well as other literary cultures touched by Arabic culture – medieval Spain, Italy and France, among others.

In common with the poetry of any warrior culture, one of the most important roles for poets of the Jahiliyya was to praise their patrons and support the martial exploits of their tribe. Zuhair however is remarkable in that his adult life was passed at a time when his tribe, the Thubian, was in continuous conflict with another group, the Aabs, yet he wrote no 'war poetry' as propaganda on behalf of his own people. Zuhair was eighty when the conflict ended after forty futile years. Zuhair's qasída praises two leaders who succeeded in resolving the pointless conflict between the Thubian and Aabs, and his remarkable ode could be considered as one of the earliest anti-conflict poems to have survived from ancient times in any culture. One of these peacemakers was inspired to work at reconciliation by the woman he loved and who refused to marry him unless he ended the war – shades of Aristophanes' Lysistrata!

In his qasída Zuhair describes a dangerous incident that threatened the 'peace process'. A brother of Hessian Ibn Thamtham was killed by a man of the Aabs tribe while negotiations were under way and Zuhair attempts to pacify both groups through his artistry; poetry was then, and in some ways remains today, the most valued artistic form for Arabic culture. Zuhair achieved his aim by praising the wisdom and status of each tribe, but also by confronting them with the horrific consequences of war. These are the lines that will probably carry most resonance for other cultures and later generations. Zuhair begins his poem with a 'nasib' in praise of a beloved, the traditional opening for qasídas. She is Leila Om-Awfa, now alienated from the poet.

Walid Abdul-Hamid and Nigel Wheale

The Mu'allaqa of Zuhair Ibn Abi Salma

Was this silent blackened site a place where Om-Awfa's tent was pitched,
    Between the rocks of Durraj and Mutathallami,
A house between her two hillside dwellings,
    The fading trace of a tattoo lost among a wrist's veins,
Here where wide-eyed antelope and deer trail each other,
    Their fawns starting up from where they lie?
I stood there again after the passage of twenty pilgrimages to Mecca,
    Hesitant and with difficulty I recognized this place,
Blackened hearth stones where cooking pots had seethed,
    The rain ditch circling the site of her tent.
Recognizing the home I saluted its ground,
    'May your morning be happy and you be safe.'

•

Look friends, do you see caravans
    Climbing the high ground above the stream of Jurthom?
Can you see the women's howdah draped with precious hangings,
    Rose-tinted veils edged with sanguine?
Among them is the one who gives pleasure to the gentle heart,
    Such pleasure to the eye craving beauty.
They started their journey at dawn and continued until late night,
    Arriving at their destination as surely as the hand to the mouth.
The mountain of Kanan was on their right
    And its rough terrain where you may meet with civil or uncivil men.
They descended to Soban and then climbed out of it,
    Their camels richly draped with Yemeni saddle cloths,
Then they left Soban climbing its peak,
    Bearing on their backs the pampered soft beauties,
Their wool caught on thorn bushes wherever they passed,
    Red as the seeds of uncrushed nightshade.
And when they arrived at the clear blue water
    They planted the staves of their longed-for camp place.
Leila' reminds me of these dreams and whoever
    Is visited by the shadows of their beloved will dream.

•

Men of Ghaiz bin Murrah have committed themselves to make peace
    After the ties between tribes had been severed in blood.
I swore an oath on the circled house of the Kaaba,
    By the men who built it from Quresh and Turhum,
I swear you are the best two masters that have ever been,
    In any time, through hardship and plenty.
You rescued the tribes of Aabs and Thubian after they
    Savaged each other, washed in the death-pledging perfume.[2]
You two said, if we reach permanent peace,
    Money and good advice will be worth the sacrifice.
So you gained the place of greatest respect,
    Above and beyond all hatred and reproach,
Great as you are in the nobility of Maad your tribe,
    You became greater as if you had opened a trove of glory.
You have distributed from your own inheritance
    Many goods, your finest marked camels.
Wounds are being healed with hundreds of beasts
    From a giver who never went to this war.
This reparation is distributed to others
    By those who never shed one drop of blood.
So who will give my message to the allied tribes
    And Thubian – did you not swear all oaths?
Do not hide any deceitful intention from God,
    Whatever is hidden from God, He knows.
It is either delayed and reserved for Judgment Day
    Or will be revenged at once.
War is the only thing you have known and tasted,
    To you the horror of it is not just an imagining.
Every time you wage war you unleash ugliness,
    When you stir it you stir a fire that burns.
Then it will grind you between millstones,
    Conceive twice each year and bear twin horrors.
It will clone children who are cursed
    Like Ahmer of Aad,[3] then breast-feed and wean them,
Like a land it will produce more horror
    Than the fertile villages of Iraq give food at harvest.

•

I swear on my life, it was the finest tribe that was wounded
    With this undeserved blow inflicted by Husain Ibn Thamtham.
He has concealed his hatred close to his chest,
    He did not reveal it, and did not hesitate,
Saying to himself, I will do what I want
    And then hide from my enemy behind a thousand warriors.
He attacked without frightening a single household,
    He delivered death where death wanted him to strike,
Near a tribe of lions fully armed
    With flaring manes and untamed claws.
Brave whenever they are wronged, they will punish
    Quickly those who wrong them and those who did not.
They took their beasts to graze and water them
    But the pool may again fill with blood and lances.
After they have achieved peace through reparation
    How could they return to the bitter inedible pastures of war?
I praise them, these two whose lances are not stained
    By the blood of Ibn Naheek or Al-Muthalam,
They did not share with their people in the blood of Nowfal
    Nor that of Wahab or of Ibn al-Muhazzami
Even though they paid the blood-money for all,
    Thousands upon thousands of healthy beasts.
They are delivered from one people to another as compensation,
    Valued herds traveling across mountains
To tribes, herds to fulfil the needs of those
    Brought down by the horror of night raids.

•

Noble people are not touched by revenge,
    Nor can anyone who wronged them escape retribution.
I've had enough of life's tribulations,
    As anyone who lives eighty years no doubt would say.
I saw death like the kicks of a blind camel,
    Whoever it hits dies, and those who are spared grow old.
And I know what today held and yesterday,
    But I am blind to what tomorrow may bring.
He who is not kind in words and dealing

Will be torn with sharp teeth and trampled by hooves.
And whoever has plenty and is miserly to his people
    Will be abandoned and cursed by them.
Whoever protects his honour through kindness will be protected
    And whoever lays himself bare to insult will be insulted.
Whoever does not protect his home will see his home destroyed
    And whoever fails to defend himself will be attacked.
Whoever fears death must inevitably confront it,
    Even if he climbs to the tracts of heaven with a ladder.
If you refuse the call of the harmless lance shaft
    The sharp force of the blade will overtake you.[4]
Whoever is faithful will not be criticized and who opens his heart
    To secure good deeds will not be slow to act.
Whoever alienates himself will create enemies from his friends,
    While whoever fails to respect himself cannot be respected.
Whatever character someone may have,
    Even if he thinks he can hide it, it will be known.
You might see a silent person whom you like,
    Yet his good and bad virtues will be revealed when he speaks.
Man is half tongue, half heart,
    What you see is an image of flesh and blood.
The feebleness of old age will never be succeeded by insight
    But the madness of youth will be followed by sanity.
We ask, you have given, and we returned and you gave again,
    But whoever demands too much may be deprived.

Notes
[1] Om-Awfa's given name.
[2] Mansham's perfume, a woman who sold fragrance in Mecca that was bought by a group of men sworn to fight to the death for their tribe.
[3] In the Qu'ran Ahmer of Aad slaughtered a holy camel, bringing disaster to his people.
[4] In desert conflicts tribes would invite conciliation before fighting by advancing the shaft of the spear, and if that failed then they advanced the blade.

Two Sonnets

Desmayarse, atreverse, estar furioso,
To faint, to hope, to become enraged,
áspero, tierno, liberal, esquivo,
Wild, tender, generous, distant,
alentado, mortal, difunto, vivo,
Brave, human, destroyed, restored,
leal, traidor, cobarde y animoso;
Loyal, deceitful, cowardly then strong;

no hallar fuera del bien centro y reposo,
To only find rest and centre in goodness,
mostrarse alegre, triste, humilde, altivo,
To seem happy, sad, modest, proud,
enojado, valiente, fugitivo,
Enraged, forward, shrinking,
satisfecho, ofendido, receloso;
Content, offended, and jealous;

huir el rostro al claro desengaño,
To turn the face from clear deception,
beber veneno por licor süave,
Drink poison for sweet wine,
olivar el provecho, amar el daño;
Shun advantage, embrace harm;

creer que un cielo en un infierno cabe,
Believe that heaven resides in hell,
dar la vida y el alma a un desengaño:
To give life and soul to deceit:
esto es amor: quien lo probó lo sabe.
All this is love, as those who feel it know.

A version from Lope de Vega

Nada es mayor que tú: sólo la rosa
Nothing is more telling than you: only the rose
tiene tu edad suspensa, ilimitada:
lives in your perfect, endless state;
eres la primavera deseada,
you are the spring I seek,
sin ser la primavera ni la rosa.
yet neither the spring nor the rose.

Vago espejo de amor donde la rosa
Obscure mirror of love where the rose
inaugura su forma deseada,
offers your wished-for form,
absorta, inmensa, pura, ilimitada,
entrancing, endless, clear, infinite
imagen, sí, pero sin ser la rosa.
vision, sure, but still not the rose.

Bajo tu piel de nube marinera,
Your skin pale like sea-horizon cloud,
luz girante tu sangre silenciosa
in a swirling light your silent blood
despliega su escarlata arborecida.
unfolds its scarlet rose grove.

Nada es mayor que tú, rosa y no rosa,
Nothing is more telling than you, rose yet no rose,
primavera sin ser la primavera;
my spring yet no spring,
arpegio en la garganta de la vida.
you the cry of song from my life's throat.

A version from Arturo Camacho Ramirez, 'Presagio del amor' (1939)

Acknowledgements

My thanks to the editors who published a number of these poems in their magazines, as editions or on websites: Tim Longville and *Grosseteste Review*; Peter Riley and Poetical Histories; Andrew Duncan and *Angel Exhaust*; Paul Green and Spectacular Diseases; Michael Haslam and *folded sheets*; Anthony Mellors and *fragmente*; Denise Riley as poetry editor for *Critical Quarterly*, and Anne Thomson of Galdragon Press. Peter Philpott brought out a first pamphlet, *Answerable Love*, from his Great Works Editions in 1977. *Strong Lines Recessional Numbers* was a fugitive pamphlet from *infernal methods* in 1980. The drawing on page [97] is heavily adapted from George Grosz, 'Be submissive to the authorities!' The epigraph to 'Elousa' on page 92 is quoted from J. H. Prynne, *High Pink on Chrome* (1975).

John Welch of The Many Press has been an inspiration and support ever since he first accepted a raw pamphlet, *Simples*, in 1979. He published *The Plains of Sight*, beautifully designed by Will Hill and including a frontispiece illustration by Harriet Dell, in 1989. The poems and interspersed prose in this sequence were read as *Madonnas of the Sign*, performances together with slide imagery and other poetry based on the life and painting of Gwen John, at the 1985 Cambridge Poetry Festival, the Tate Gallery, July 1985, the Barbican Art Gallery to accompany the retrospective exhibition *Gwen John: An Interior Life*, October 1985, and Southampton Art Gallery, with Ray Smith, painter, *Exploring the Works of Gwen John*, February 1987. Italicized quotations between speech marks in the sequence are taken or lightly adapted from Mary Taubman, *Gwen John*, (Scolar Press, 1985) and Cecily Langdale and David Fraser Jenkins, *Gwen John: An Interior Life*, (Phaidon Press and Barbican Art Gallery, 1985). A. D. Fraser Jenkins, *Gwen John at the National Museum of Wales*, (Cardiff, 1976) was read for description of drawing and painting technique.

John Welch also published *The Windshield Glarestrip Legends*, *Strong Lines Recessional Numbers*, *From the Versts*, *As if from the Russian*, *New York/ Warsaw Transfers*, and a shorter version of *Hearing and Calling*, in *Phrasing the Light*, 1994, design and typography by Ewan Smith. The ink drawing for 'Phrasing the Light' by Dan Wheale appears here on page [31].

It has been a privilege and a collaborative joy to work with Dr Walid Abdul-Hamid translating the qasídas of al-Mutanabbí and Zuhair, a continuing project. Peter Riley published 'He said to his Prince and Patron Sayf al-Dawla' as Poetical Histories No. 56 in 2002. Michael Schmidt published several of the translations in *PN Review* 134 (2002) together with the introductory note, and Zuhair's qasída on reconciliation was read on BBC Radio Four's *Poetry Please*, 10 November 2003.

The glyphs on page [9] were reproduced as the cover image for *Flows and Traces*, *(infernal methods @ thule*, 2004) and are thought to be Neolithic marks, 0.19 metres high, found on a flagstone slab lining the north side of the south-west pier within Maes Howe chambered tomb, Orkney, c. 3000 BCE. See P. J. Ashmore, 'Neolithic carvings in Maes Howe', *Proceedings of the Society of Antiquaries of Scotland*, vol. 16 (1986), pp. 57–62. For the image on page 30 see H. F. Morland Simpson, 'A Scandinavian Stave Calendar (sometime belonging to J. W. Cursiter Esq.), now in Skaill House, Sandwick, Orkney', *New Orkney Antiquarian Journal*, vol. 2 (2002), pp. 49–60. The 'S'-marked stave notates summer, the unmarked stave winter. This sequence of poems was made for *Flows & Traces*, a group exhibition of writing, sculpture, collage and photography, working with Yvonne Gray, Malcolm Olva and Frances Pelly, and shown at the Loft Gallery, St Margaret's Hope, South Ronaldsay, Orkney, November–December 2004, and reprised in The Back Room, Waterfront Gallery, Stromness, February–March 2005, with thanks to Trudi Hall, all organizers and funding organizations.

For the cover artwork, many thanks to Calum Morrison of Stromness for his colour rhapsody of Flotta refinery on a rough day, to Henry Hall for digitizing the image, and to Andrew Jones for file transfer. And final thanks to Tony Frazer of Shearsman for this entire opportunity.

CPSIA information can be obtained at www.ICGtesting.com
Printed in the USA
LVOW12s0037160913

352566LV00001B/358/A